PLASTICS

Jacqueline Dineen

The story of plastics—what they are, how they are made, and the thousands of uses to which they are put.

ENSLOW PUBLISHERS, INC.
Bloy St & Ramsey Ave.
Box 777
Hillside, N.J. 07205

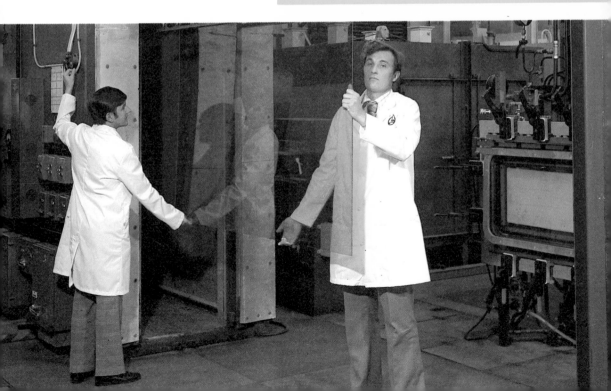

Contents

In the picture above, the girl's ski-suit is made of plastic fibres.
[cover] The cover picture shows a children's nursery in which the exciting colours are produced with plastic paints.
[title page] The picture on the title page shows a sheet of Perspex being loaded into an oven.
[1–24] All other pictures are identified by number in the text.

LIBRARY OF CONGRESS
Library of Congress Cataloging-in-Publication Data
Dineen, Jacqueline.
    Plastics / Jacqueline Dineen.
        p.   cm. -- (The world's harvest)
    Includes index.
    Summary: Explains what plastics are, how they are made, and their many uses.
    ISBN 0-89490-221-0
    1. Plastics--Juvenile literature. [1. Plastics.] I. Title.
II. Series: Dineen, Jacqueline. World's harvest.
TA455.P5D56 1988
668.4--dc19   88-3550
                                                        CIP
                                                        AC

Introduction

It is amazing to think that your grandparents never saw plastic when they were children. When they were babies they ate their food off plates made of china or metal, nothing like those delightful ones in picture [1].

Plastics are made by man from chemicals. These chemicals come from oil. Don't be frightened by the word 'chemicals'. Everything in the world is made of chemicals—even you!

In chapter 1 I tell you what plastic is. I describe some of the early plastic materials like celluloid and Bakelite, and I tell you the difference between the two main groups of plastics—thermoplastics, and thermosetting plastics.

In chapter 2, I describe how plastics are

[1]

A refinery is a place where crude oil is sent to be refined. 'Refining' means turning a substance into a pure state, with all unwanted parts removed.

made today. I begin with the oil being treated at the refinery to separate the different chemicals. I explain how a tough material like polythene is made from a gas.

Moulding and laminating

Many plastic articles are shaped by a process called 'moulding' and I tell you about this in chapter 3. There are different methods of moulding to make things like washing-up bowls and kitchenware, long lengths like curtain rails and drainpipes, and hollow articles like plastic bottles.

In chapter 4, I tell you about some items which don't have to be shaped—laminates like the ones used to make kitchen worktops, and the plastic sheets and films used to wrap food in the supermarket. I also tell you about a process called 'vacuum forming' which is used to make the plastic cups in a vending machine.

Did you know that paints and glues contain plastic? I tell you about this in chapter 5. In chapter 6, I talk about two quite different plastics—plastic foam, and plastics which are reinforced with glass fibres.

If you look at the labels inside your clothes you will probably find that they are made from man-made fibres, or a blend of natural and man-made fibres. In the last chapter, I tell you about these man-made fibres and how they are made.

Man-made fibres are fibres which are not produced from natural materials like wool, silk, or cotton, but are manufactured from chemicals.

That completes the story of plastic and all the things that are made from it. It is an interesting story because it is such a big part of our world today.

1 · *What is plastic?*

Have you ever made a model out of modelling clay, or a flour-and-water mixture? These things are soft and can be moulded into any shape. They are 'plastic'. That is what the word means—something which can be moulded or shaped.

The name 'plastics' is given to a huge range of man-made materials which can be shaped when heated and then made to keep their shape. Everywhere we go these days we see

[2]

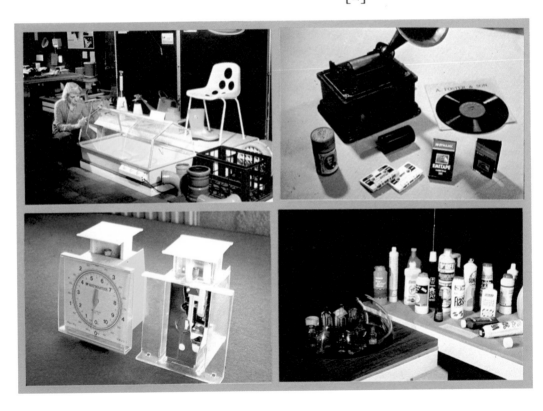

plastic. If you look around your home, your school, and the shops you visit, you will see hundreds of things made of plastic. For instance, your hands are touching plastic at this moment. Yes they are! The cover of this book has a very, very thin sheet of plastic stuck on to it, to give it a nice shiny appearance, and to keep it clean. Picture [2] shows a tiny selection of the variety of plastic things in our world.

As plastics are entirely man-made, you might think they do not belong in a series called 'The World's Harvest'. But plastics are made from chemicals which come from natural products like oil, gas, and coal.

Chemicals are not mysterious things found only in a scientist's laboratory. They are all around us. The air we breathe, plants and trees, even our own bodies, are made up of chemical 'elements'. There are about one hundred chemical elements altogether. Some examples are carbon, oxygen, hydrogen, sodium, and sulphur. You have probably heard of some of these. Perhaps you can name others.

Plastics are made by mixing together the atoms of these various elements. (Atoms are the tiny particles of which all matter is formed; they are much too small to be seen even with a microscope.)

Every plastic object you see is made by forming compounds (mixtures) of atoms. It never happens naturally. Engineers have to make it happen.

The first man-made plastic was called celluloid. It was introduced in 1862. Celluloid is made from the woody part of plants, such as

cotton fibre or the wood pulp used in paper-making.

The next development was cellulose acetate, which is still used to make spectacle frames, artificial fibres, and clear film.

In America a chemist called Leo Baekeland found out how to make a new sort of plastic—Bakelite. It was the real forerunner of modern plastics.

Bakelite was the first example of a 'thermosetting' plastic. Thermosetting plastics are hard and rigid. They are used to make articles like electrical fittings and saucepan handles. You can see a selection of Bakelite fittings in picture [3]. The plastic is heated

Thermoplastics and thermosetting plastics

7

[4]

PVC is a thermoplastic resin made from a chemical called polyvinyl chloride. It provides resistance to water, acids, and other liquids.

until it is soft and shapeable. When it has been moulded it is heated again until it hardens, keeping the shape it has been given. Once' it has hardened it cannot be softened again. The thermosetting plastics include melamine, polyester resins, and polyurethane. They can be used to make all sorts of things from cups and saucers to car bodies and boat hulls.

The other type of plastics is called 'thermoplastics'. Polythene and PVC are both well-known examples of thermoplastics. Like thermosetting plastics they become soft when they are heated, but they are not heated again to harden them. They harden and keep their shape when they are cooled, but they become soft again every time they are re-heated. They can be heated, re-shaped, and cooled into a solid time after time. Picture [4] shows kitchen containers made of polythene.

Polythene and PVC were first made in the 1930s. Since then many new plastics have been invented.

Most modern plastics are made from chemicals found in petroleum. In the next chapter I explain how these plastics are made.

2 · *Making plastics today*

Oil is one of our most valuable natural products. The crude oil (petroleum) which comes out of the ground contains a lot of useful chemicals. It is taken to a refinery, where it is separated into different parts by a process called distillation.

Distillation is a method of separating liquids with different boiling temperatures. When a liquid boils, it gradually turns into a vapour. When this vapour cools it condenses back into liquid. You can see this when you boil a kettle. As the water boils, steam comes out of the kettle. If the steam hits a cold object such as a wall, it turns back into drops of water.

You can see a refinery and chemical plant in picture [5]. There the petroleum is heated at

[5]

the bottom of the tall tower. All the chemicals in the petroleum boil at different temperatures. The ones with the lowest boiling temperatures boil first, and remain boiling for longest. The vapours from these travel right up the tower before they cool. The vapours from the chemicals with higher boiling points do not float up so far. They cool and condense at lower levels. There are trays at different heights in the tower to collect the different liquids as they form.

Oil products like petrol, diesel oil, paraffin, and lubricating oils are separated in this way. The chemicals for making plastics are all obtained at the same time. One of the most important of these chemicals is ethylene, which is used to make polythene. In its natural form, ethylene is a gas. Let us see how it ends up as a tough plastic.

Molecules and chains

Two or more atoms joined together are called a molecule. Molecules are called small or large depending on how many atoms they contain.

I want you to imagine a crowd of people at a railway station. Some are running to catch trains, some are meeting people, some are buying magazines. The molecules in ethylene gas look a bit like that! They are moving around haphazardly in all directions. Now imagine that some of those people queue up to buy tickets. This queue (or chain) of people looks a bit like a polythene molecule. What the scientists do to make the molecules in the gas form a chain is to add another chemical called a 'catalyst'.

A catalyst is any substance which causes a chemical change to something (but is not changed itself in the process).

[6]

In picture [6] you can see a model (millions of times enlarged) of a chain of polythene molecules. The picture also shows samples of polythene objects.

Now let's go back to that railway station. More people form more queues. Some are queuing for newspapers, some are queuing for cups of coffee, some are queuing up for taxis. All over the station there are chains of people, and these chains begin to cross over each other and get tangled up. Now they look like the molecules in a piece of polythene. These chains and the way they tangle together are what gives plastic its special properties.

Thermoplastics such as polythene have particularly long molecules. When the plastic is cool, the molecules lie together and are still. When the plastic is heated, the molecules start to move apart and the material becomes soft and pliable. When the plastic is cooled again,

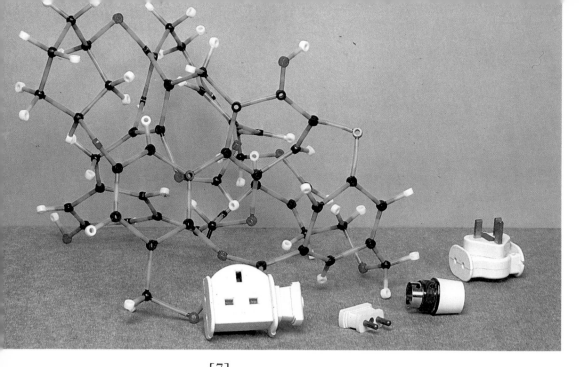

[7]

the molecules move back together and the material hardens.

Thermosetting plastics are made in a similar way, but the molecules are shorter. The molecules move apart when the plastic is heated, like thermoplastics. When the plastic is heated even more, however, the molecules start to react with each other and form links. These strong links make the material set hard and it can never be softened and reshaped. The model in picture [7] shows what a molecule of thermosetting plastic looks like. It also shows samples of electric plugs which are made of thermosetting plastic.

Ethylene is not only used to make polythene. It can be changed into other·chemicals to make different plastics such as PVC, polystyrene, and polyurethane.

3 · Moulding plastics

There are several ways of moulding plastics.
Remember what I said about the difference
between thermosetting plastics and
thermoplastics? Articles from thermosetting
plastics are made by a method called
'compression moulding'. A steel mould, made
in two parts, is used for this. When the two
parts are fitted together, the space inside is the
shape and size of the article being made.

The mould is fitted to a press. The press can

A mould is a hollow shape, inside
which objects are made so that
they take on the same shape. (Or
the shape might be *solid* and the
shape is constructed *around* it.)

[8]

be opened to separate the two parts or closed to push them together. Sometimes the plastic is coloured with a dye before it is put into the mould.

The material for moulding may be in the form of powder, granules, or a large pellet. It is measured out and put on to the lower part of the mould. The press is closed and the mould heats up. The heat passes to the plastic, making it soft. The pressure on it forces it into every part of the mould. The moulding is left to harden in the heat. Then the press is opened and the moulding is taken out.

Injection moulding

There are various ways of making articles from thermoplastics. One method is called injection moulding. You can see an injection moulding machine in picture [8]. Granules of plastic material are fed into a heated horizontal tube

[10]

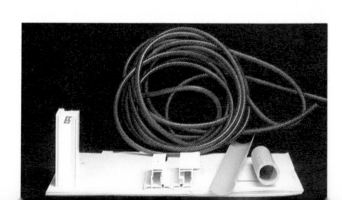

with a revolving screw inside. The heat in the tube softens the material. As the screw turns, it forces the soft plastic along the tube and out into a cold, closed mould where it cools down and hardens. The mould is then opened and the moulding taken out. In picture [9] you can see an opened mould and the finished, moulded object taken out of it.

There is a similar method which is used to make long continuous articles like the curtain rails, ipes, guttering, and garden hoses in pictu e [10]. It is called extrusion.

Look at the extrusion machine in picture [11]. The material is heated in a horizontal

Extrusion moulding

[11]

tube and extruded (forced out) through a hole at one end. It does not go into a mould, but comes out as a continuous length shaped like the hole in the tube. As it comes out of the tube, the plastic is cooled by cold air or water. It hardens and keeps its shape.

Blow moulding

Plastic bottles and other hollow objects are made by a method called 'blow moulding'. First, an extrusion machine is used to produce a continuous hollow tube of plastic material. A mould closes round the plastic. At the same time, a jet of cold air is blown through the middle of the tube, forcing the plastic against the sides of the mould. The cold air cools the material so that it hardens in the shape of the mould.

Moulding is the most common method of shaping plastics. Find all the different plastic articles you can and see if you can work out which moulding method was used to make them. You will find plenty of things in the kitchen—buckets, bowls, storage containers, fittings on the washing machine and cooker and inside the refrigerator, electrical gadgets like mixers and blenders, the handles of saucepans. Elsewhere in the house don't forget the telephone, knobs, switches, screw caps on bottles, the cap on the toothpaste tube, the PVC records you put on your record player, the trimming on metal articles. Whatever did people do before plastics existed!

4 · *Laminates, sheets, and film*

If you go into your kitchen at home, you will probably see worktops of a plastic material. They are probably made of a plastic laminate.

Laminates are made by pressing thin layers of material together into a hard, strong sheet.

First, layers of paper or cloth are soaked in a solution containing thermosetting resin. The sheets are piled up and put between two steel plates. The whole sandwich is then put into a heated press and squeezed tightly together. The heat softens the resin, which flows and then sets into a hard, rigid sheet.

The resin is usually Bakelite or melamine. Melamine can be dyed to make coloured laminates. Decorative worktops like the one in picture [12] are made by printing a design on the top sheet of paper or cloth and then

Resin is a liquid plastic. It is called resin because it looks like the natural resin which oozes out of certain plants, especially pines.

[12]

covering it with a very thin layer of paper containing transparent melamine resin. The resin protects the design without hiding it.

Large amounts of plastic laminate are made on factory machines. At one end of the production line is a big roll of paper or fabric. This material passes through a bath of plastic resin solution. Then it is 'wrung out' between rollers, dried in a drying tunnel, cut into lengths, and put into the press.

Plastic laminates are very useful in the kitchen because they are tough and heat resistant. This means that they do not scorch or melt if hot objects are put on them.

Perspex

Another type of plastic sheet is called Perspex. Perspex is not a laminate. It is a clear plastic, like unbreakable glass, which is made by the 'casting' method.

Perspex is a thermoplastic. A chemical is heated with a catalyst until it turns into a sticky liquid. This liquid is then poured into a casting cell made of two flat pieces of glass. The sheets of glass are clamped tightly together and passed through an oven like the one shown on the title page of this book. The cell is then allowed to cool before the clamps are removed.

Flexible plastic sheeting

Laminated and Perspex sheets are rigid. Different methods are used to make flexible plastic sheets. Plastic shower curtains and light raincoats, for example, are made from PVC.

PVC would be too brittle on its own, so it is

[13]

mixed with a substance called a plasticizer.
The plasticizer may be a liquid or a liquid
plastic resin. Other ingredients such as
colouring pigments are added to the mixture.

The PVC mixture is made into sheeting on a
machine called a calender. A calender is like a
big mangle, with four or five horizontal rollers
arranged one above the other in a zig-zag
formation. The rollers are heated by steam or
hot oil and the plastic material is squeezed into
a thin sheet between them.

If you walk round a supermarket, you will
notice that a lot of the food is packaged in
clear plastic film. Loose items like potatoes are
sold in plastic bags. Other items are sold in
decorated packets, like those potato crisps in
picture [13]. The clear plastic protects the food
from handling by shoppers, yet allows them to

A plasticizer is a substance added
to plastics, mortar, and similar
mixtures, to make it soft and
sticky.

[14]

see what they are buying. The usual plastic for this purpose is polythene.

Plastic films and sheets are made in several ways, but the method used most is a version of extrusion called the 'tubular film process'. The plastic material is extruded in a long thin tube. A jet of cold air is blown through the tube, making it blow up like a balloon. If you blow up a balloon, the rubber becomes much thinner as it stretches. The same thing happens with the film. The thin, expanded film is cooled and flattened out between rollers, as you can see happening in picture [14]. It is then wound on to reels.

Some foods and other articles are 'shrink-wrapped'. Plastic film is heated and stretched. When it cools, it stays stretched. The film is wrapped around the article and sealed. It then goes through a hot tunnel which makes the plastic soft again. It shrinks to its original size, encasing the article very tightly.

If you buy a drink from a vending machine,

it will come in a plastic cup. These cups are made from plastic sheets by a method called 'vacuum forming'. Vacuum forming is a useful process for making shaped packaging which does not have to last too long. Foods like yogurt, cream, and margarine often come in vacuum-formed containers. It is also used to package some toys and household articles.

The plastic sheet is clamped to the top of a mould. It is heated until it becomes soft. A vacuum pump sucks air out through very fine holes in the bottom of the mould. The soft plastic is forced down until it covers the surface of the mould. It is cooled and hardens in the shape of the mould.

Vacuum forming from very thick plastic sheets is used to make articles like plastic baths. Picture [15] shows a plastic sheet lying across the mould. In picture [16] the sheet has been sucked down into the shape of a bath.

[15]   [16]

5 · *Paints and adhesives*

Did you know that paint contains plastic? Paint has three main parts. The first is a pigment which gives it colour and hides the surface underneath. The second is a hard transparent resin which holds the pigment in place and gives it a protective surface. The third is a solvent (a dissolving substance) which makes the resin flow to give a smooth surface. It also thins the paint so that it is easier to apply. When the paint has been applied, the solvent evaporates and the resin dries.

Paints used to include natural resins such as rosin from pine trees, but nowadays they are normally plastic. Gloss paints, like those in picture [17], for covering the woodwork in your house, contain resin. Paints for cars and bicycles are made with a slightly different resin to give them a very hard, glossy finish that will not chip too easily, and will stand up to bad weather.

The solvent is usually a liquid such as white spirit, which comes from petroleum. The resin is dissolved in the solvent and the pigment is ground in to give a smooth mixture.

Emulsion paint, for painting the walls of your house, is made with PVA and water. As the water evaporates, the mixture forms into a PVA film.

If you are painting your house, you put on the paint with a brush and it dries naturally. Cars and bicycles, however, are painted by dipping them in a vat of paint, or by putting

PVA is a thermoplastic resin made from a chemical called polyvinyl acetate. It is used as an adhesive in inks, etc.

the paint on with a spray gun. They then pass
through an oven heated to about 120°C. The
solvent evaporates and the resin sets to a hard,
glossy finish.

Clear varnishes are made in a similar way,
but no colouring pigment is added to the
solvent and resin.

[17]

Most glues nowadays are made from plastic
resins. They are very strong and will stick
almost any material together. Adhesives made
from a group of thermosetting plastics called
epoxy resins will stick metal, glass, china,
plastics, and—as you see in picture [18]—
wood.

Adhesives

23

[18]

Plastic resins are used to make plywood and chipboard from wood. Plywood is made from thin flat sheets of wood stuck together with resin glue. The grain of the wood is laid at right-angles to the grain on the layer below, which makes the plywood very strong. Chipboard is made by coating small chips of wood with a resin adhesive and then pressing them tightly together in a heated press. The thermosetting resins harden to give a very strong and permanent bond.

Plastic resins are also used to strengthen some types of paper. Paper disintegrates when it gets wet, so paper articles which have to stand up to water have a small amount of resin in them. Paper tissues and kitchen towels are made by mixing a specially prepared resin into the paper pulp. Then the pulp is made into sheets and dried. The resin hardens and holds the fibres in the paper firmly together, even when the paper gets wet.

6 · *Foam and glass fibre*

Plastic is not used only in its solid form. It can also be filled with air bubbles to make plastic foam. Plastic foam is a useful material for insulating, packaging, and for making soft furnishings. The bubbles make it an excellent heat insulator.

When you turn on the fire in a house that has not been insulated, a lot of the heat escapes through the walls and the roof. Plastic foam insulation helps to prevent this heat loss.

Most houses have an inner and an outer wall, with a cavity (space) between. If foam is pumped into this cavity it prevents heat from inside the house escaping through the walls. You can see this being done in picture [19].

There are two types of plastic foam. One is the flexible spongy sort used in upholstery, cushions, and mattresses. The other is a rigid foam which is mainly used for heat insulation.

Some plastic foams are made from a thermosetting plastic called polyurethane.

[19]

Polyurethanes are made by mixing two liquid chemicals with a catalyst to form a rubbery plastic. To make plastic foam, a foaming agent is added to the polyurethane mixture. When this foaming agent is heated it gives off a gas which fills the mixture with bubbles and makes it expand. The plastic sets into a flexible, spongy foam.

Flexible foam can be used in all sorts of ways. It is light and soft so it makes comfortable furniture and car seats. Foam linings in coats and other clothes make them warmer. Thin strips are used as draught excluders round doors and windows, and small pieces make paint rollers and artificial sponges. Some carpets have a foam backing to make them more springy, and delicate articles may be packed in foam to protect them on their journey from factory to shop.

Rigid foam

Rigid foam is made from specially prepared polyurethane or from other thermosetting resins. The resin is mixed very hard with an acid and a foaming agent so that it froths up and sets almost instantly. The mass of bubbles surrounded by solid resin gives a rigid, lightweight foam.

Rigid foams made from polyurethane can be shaped so that they go round hot water pipes to stop heat escaping. Slabs of foam are also used as heat insulators in refrigerators and freezers for the opposite reason—they prevent the heat getting *in*.

Polystyrene is a brittle, transparent thermoplastic used for making kitchen

equipment such as see-through storage jars and measuring jugs. Fridges are often lined with a specially toughened polystyrene.

Expanded polystyrene is a very lightweight, rigid plastic made by heating tiny beads of polystyrene with a foaming agent. A gas is released, and the mixture foams up into a very light mass filled with bubbles. It is often used for ceiling tiles, which prevent heat loss. It is also used for packaging fragile articles like the bottles and glasses in picture [20].

Reinforcing with glass fibres

Most reinforced plastics are made from a thermosetting material called polyester resin, which is waterproof. It is reinforced with sheets made from chopped glass fibres. First, a mould is made in the shape of the required article. Then a mixture containing liquid polyester resin is sprayed on and allowed to set. A glass fibre mat is added, and a layer of the liquid polyester mixture is rolled into it. It is allowed to set hard before the next layer of glass fibre is added. Layers are built up in this way until the correct thickness is obtained. Picture [21] shows what the glass fibre and liquid polyester look like.

Glass reinforced plastic is used in many ways because it is strong, light, and does not rust or rot. Pigments can be added to the polyester to give it colour and make it opaque. Boats, garden pools, and parts of car bodies are just some of the things made with this material. Translucent sheets are used for roofing material in factories and other buildings like the one in picture [22] where plenty of light is needed.

[21]

[22]

7 · *Man-made fibres*

If you look at the labels inside your clothes, you will see that some of them are made of materials like nylon, polyester, and acrylic. These are man-made fibres, and they are made from plastic. The girl on page 2 is wearing a ski-suit made from man-made fibres.

The first man-made fibre, acetate, was developed in the 1920s and nylon was introduced in America a few years later.

There are two types of man-made fibre. 'Regenerated' fibres are made from natural substances which are changed by the addition of chemicals. Acetate and viscose are two of the regenerated fibres.

The other type is the synthetic fibres which are made entirely from chemicals. The best known synthetic fibres are nylon and acrylic. The materials used for making synthetic fibres are thermoplastics, which are made into fibres by extrusion.

The most usual extrusion method is called melt spinning. The hard plastic is melted into a liquid and forced through very fine holes in a machine called a spinneret. It comes out in long threads, or filaments, which are cooled so that they harden.

There are two other methods of making synthetic fibres. The first is called wet spinning, which is used to make viscose and some acrylics. As the filaments come out of the

Melt spinning, wet spinning, and dry spinning

29

spinneret they pass straight into a chemical bath which makes them solidify.

Acetate and most acrylics are made by dry spinning. The plastic material is dissolved in a solvent which evaporates in warm air when the filaments come out of the spinneret. The filaments are then spun into yarn in the same way as cotton. In picture [23] samples of dyed fibre are being combed so that they can be tested for quality. The yarn is woven on looms like the one in picture [24], on which fabric for sacks and carpet backing is being made.

Man-made fibres are used a great deal these days. One reason is that there is not enough natural fibre like wool and cotton to go round. Another reason is that they are cheaper to produce, and the clothes made from them are easier to look after. They do not crease so readily, they do not shrink in the wash, and they are easier to iron; often they need no ironing at all.

A lot of clothes (and other fabric articles like carpets and furniture coverings) are made from a blend of natural and man-made fibres. Cotton is often blended with acrylic, or wool with polyester. In that way the warmth and the nice feel of the natural fabric is combined with the advantages of the man-made fibre.

Look around your house and see how much 'plastic cloth' you can find. Sheets, blankets, duvets, curtains, carpets, and upholstery probably have man-made fibres in them. Some will be made entirely of man-made fibres. They may not look it, but they are just as plastic as the washing up bowl in the kitchen.

'Everything is plastic these days,' people

[23]

[24]

sometimes complain. They mean that things are artificial, or all look the same. Now that you have read this book you can decide for yourself if you agree with them.

Index

Acknowledgements for photographs: Berger Paints, picture on cover and no. 17; BIP Chemicals 1, 22; Bostik (Emhart Chemical Group) 18; BP Chemicals 3, 4, 5, 20; Courtaulds 23; Education Service of the Plastics Industry 2, 6, 7, 8, 9, 10, 11, 12, 21; Homewarm 19; ICI Fibres, picture on Contents page; ICI Plastics Division, picture on Title page and nos, 13, 14, 15, 16, 24.